Haggadah for Chris
Celebrating a Christ-Centered

by Eitan Bar

Copyright © 2024

ISBN 9798871591727

www.eitan.bar

Scan for a complimentary bonus:

Or visit: www.eitan.bar/passover

Introduction

Tonight, we joyfully gather to participate in a Passover Seder. "SEDER," a Hebrew term, signifies "the order of service," guiding us through this vibrant and meaningful celebration.

For countless generations, the Passover story has been brought to life through the Haggadah. This sacred compilation, whose name means "the telling," is rich with liturgy, stories, shared readings, and scriptural insights. It serves as a beacon, illuminating Jewish families in their observance of this revered festival. Across the globe, myriad Haggadah versions from diverse Jewish cultures recount the tale of God's deliverance of the Israelites from Egyptian bondage, each narrating a unique facet of this miraculous redemption.

Our guide for tonight's observance is a special Haggadah, a term rooted in the Hebrew verb "to tell," as echoed in Exodus 13:8: *"On that day tell your son, 'I do this because of what the LORD did for me when I came out of Egypt.'"*

This Haggadah is distinctive for two key reasons. Firstly, it diverges from the classical Jewish Haggadah by omitting sections that traditionally express disdain towards Jesus and his followers. Secondly, it intertwines the ancient narrative of liberation from Egyptian slavery with the celebration of our spiritual redemption through Messiah Yeshua (Jesus Christ).

In keeping with Jewish tradition, each generation is encouraged to envision themselves as personally liberated from Egyptian servitude. Yet, as followers of Jesus, our journey extends beyond the sands of ancient Egypt to a spacious upper room in Jerusalem. There, during the time of Jesus, we will symbolically partake in the inauguration of the New Covenant, uniting past and present in a profound act of faith and remembrance.

Chag Sameach!
(Happy Passover)

Everyone:

Chag Sameach!
(Happy Passover)

Preparation

In the spirited days leading up to Passover, a devout Jewish family engages in a thorough search of their home, meticulously removing all leavened items – anything containing yeast. This ritual echoes the Biblical mandate for the Feast of Unleavened Bread, as detailed in Exodus 12:19-29:

"For seven days no yeast is to be found in your houses. And whoever eats anything with yeast in it must be cut off from the community of Israel, whether he is an alien or native-born. Eat nothing made with yeast. Wherever you live, you must eat unleavened bread."

As believers in Jesus, we find profound meaning in these traditions. The Scriptures often use leaven as a metaphor for sin, as eloquently stated in the Epistle to the Corinthians:

"Don't you know that a little yeast works through the whole batch of dough? Get rid of the old yeast that you may be a new batch without yeast—as you really are. For Christ, our Passover lamb, has been sacrificed. Therefore let us keep the Festival, not with the old yeast, the yeast of malice and wickedness, but with bread without yeast, the bread of sincerity and truth." (1 Corinthians 5:6-7)

In accordance with the Biblical commandment, Yeshua (Jesus) made preparations to observe the Passover:

> *Then came the day of Unleavened Bread on which the Passover lamb had to be sacrificed. Jesus sent Peter and John, saying, "Go and make preparations for us to eat the Passover."*
>
> *"Where do you want us to prepare for it?" they asked.*
>
> *He replied, "As you enter the city, a man carrying a jar of water will meet you. Follow him to the house that he enters, 11 and say to the owner of the house, 'The Teacher asks: Where is the guest room, where I may eat the Passover with my disciples?' He will show you a large room upstairs, all furnished. Make preparations there."*
>
> *They left and found things just as Jesus had told them. So they prepared the Passover. (Luke 22:7-13)*

Tonight, we will commemorate the Passover Seder together!

Birkat HaNer – Kindling of the Candles

 A female participant is required, preferably the head of the household, who may also be the mother.

Leader:

As [the mother's name] kindles light to begin the Seder, let us joyfully recall how the Lord chose a woman to bring forth our Messiah, the Light of the world. This act, rich in symbolism, reminds us of the divine light that guides and enriches our lives.

Mother:

 Blessed are you, O Lord our God, King of the universe, Who has sanctified us with Thy commandments and commanded us to be a light to the nations and Who gave us Yeshua our Messiah the light of the word in whose Name we light the festival lights.

Everyone:

Amen!

The Four Cups

The Passover Seder unfolds through four ceremonial cups of the fruit of the vine, each anchoring a distinct part of the experience. These cups are named in honor of the four promises God made to Israel in Exodus 6:6–7. Every cup symbolically aligns with a different phase in the Seder's progression, weaving a tapestry of tradition and narrative that enriches our celebration:

1. The Cup of Sanctification
2. The Cup of Plagues
3. The Cup of Redemption
4. The Cup of Praise

 Tip: *Drinking wine during the Seder is known to significantly increase your enjoyment and enhance your singing abilities!*

 Tip: *Children (and Baptists) can drink grape juice instead.*

Kiddush – First Cup: The Cup of Sanctification

The Seder commences with the Cup of Sanctification, also known as the Cup of Blessing. This inaugural cup sets the tone for the evening, marking it as a sacred and holy time. In line with Jewish tradition, we fill our cups to the brim, signifying overflowing joy. Passover is a time to revel in God's kindness and celebrate the freedom He granted us in Christ.

> *When the hour came, Jesus and his apostles reclined at the table. And he said to them, "I have eagerly desired to eat this Passover with you before I suffer. For I tell you, I will not eat it again until it finds fulfillment in the kingdom of God." After taking the cup, he gave thanks (recited the blessing) and said, "Take this and divide it among you. For I tell you I will not drink again of the fruit of the vine until the kingdom of God comes." (Luke 22:14-18)*

According to Jewish tradition, we drink from the cup while comfortably reclining to the left.

[Everyone fills their cup. Lift up the cup. Leaning to the left.]

Everyone:

" ***Blessed are you, O Lord our God, King of the universe, Creator of the fruit of the vine.***

Amen!

Urchatz – Washing of the Hands

During the Passover celebration, the first washing of hands is a symbolic act of personal sanctification. Typically, two children carry a pitcher, a basin, and a towel and go around the table pouring a little water on the guests' hands or allowing them to dip their hands. The washing starts with the leader of the Seder and is meant to symbolically purify oneself before the holy celebration.

[While the guests wash their hands, the leader reads:]

After that, he poured water into a basin and began to wash his disciples' feet, drying them with the towel that was wrapped around him. When he had finished washing their feet, he put on his clothes and returned to his place. "Do you understand what I have done for you?" he asked them. "You call me 'Teacher' and 'Lord,' and rightly so, for that is what I am. Now that I, your Lord and Teacher, have washed your feet, you also should wash one another's feet. (John 13:5, 12-14)

Karpas – Dipping of the Parsley

Leader:

The wine we savor, rich and red, symbolizes the blood of the Passover Lamb. Similarly, this parsley embodies the hyssop the Israelites used to apply the lamb's blood to their doorframes (Exodus 12:22). The saltwater, meanwhile, represents the tears shed in Egypt, a poignant reminder of the pain, suffering, and sorrow endured there. As we dip a sprig of parsley into the salt water, let us reflect on how life is often mingled with tears yet carries the promise of redemption and hope.

[Everyone takes a piece of parsley, recite the blessing, then eat.]

Everyone:

 Blessed are you, O Lord our God, King of the universe, Creator of the fruit of the earth.

Amen!

Yachatz – Breaking of the Middle Matzah

Leader:

Matzah (unleavened bread) is a key element of Passover. During the Seder, three matzah sheets are placed in a three-compartment bag known as the matzah tash. This tripartite arrangement holds rich symbolism in Jewish tradition. It may represent the three Patriarchs: Abraham, Isaac, and Jacob, or the divisions within the people of Israel: the priests, the Levites, and the general populace. Believers in Yeshua (Jesus) often view it as a symbol of the Trinity: the Father, the Son, and the Holy Spirit.

Maggid – The Story of the Passover

Exodus 12:1-13, to be read by a guest

Guest:

" *The Lord said to Moses and Aaron in Egypt, "This month is to be for you the first month, the first month of your year. Tell the whole community of Israel that on the tenth day of this month each man is to take a lamb for his family, one for each household. If any household is too small for a whole lamb, they must share one with their nearest neighbor, having taken into account the number of people there are. You are to determine the amount of lamb needed in accordance with what each person will eat. The animals you choose must be year-old males without defect, and you may take them from the sheep or the goats. Take care of them until the fourteenth day of the month, when all the members of the community of Israel must slaughter them at twilight. Then they are to take some of the blood and put it on the sides and tops of the doorframes of the houses where they eat the lambs. That same night they are to eat the meat roasted over the fire, along with bitter herbs, and bread made without yeast. Do not eat the meat raw or boiled in water, but roast it over a fire—with the head, legs and internal organs. Do not leave any of it till morning; if some is left till morning, you must burn it. This is how you are to eat it: with your cloak tucked into your belt, your sandals on your feet and your staff in your hand. Eat it in haste; it is the Lord's Passover.*

On that same night I will pass through Egypt and strike down every firstborn of both people and animals, and I will bring judgment on all the gods of Egypt. I am the Lord. The blood will be a sign for you on the houses where you are, and when I see the blood, I will pass over you. No destructive plague will touch you when I strike Egypt."

Ma-Nishtanah – The Four Questions

As we commence the retelling of the Exodus story, the youngest child (able to read) poses the Four Questions to the Seder leader.

 Tip: *You may opt for all the children to read them in unison or assign each question to a different child.*

Youngest Guest/s:

"Why is this night different from all other nights?...

...On all other nights we eat either leavened or unleavened bread; why on this night do we eat only matzah which is unleavened bread?"

"On all other nights we eat vegetables and herbs of all kinds; why on this night do we eat only bitter herbs?"

"On all other nights we never think of dipping herbs in water or in anything else; why on this night do we dip the parsley in salt water and the bitter herbs in charoseth?"

"On all other nights we eat either sitting upright or reclining why on this night do we all recline?"

The leader of the Seder responds with the traditional answer...

I'm delighted you asked these questions. This night stands apart, as we commemorate the Jewish people's transition from slavery to freedom.

Why do we eat only matzah tonight?

When Israel fled Egypt, they had to leave swiftly. There was no time to bake their bread or wait for the yeast to rise. The scorching sun baked their dough into unleavened bread, known as matzah, as they journeyed.

Why do we eat bitter herbs tonight?

Israel endured harsh slavery in Egypt, and their lives were filled with bitterness, which these herbs represent.

Why do we dip the herbs twice tonight?

We dip parsley in salt water, symbolizing the hope of spring. The bitter herbs are dipped in sweet charoset, reflecting how the hope of freedom sweetened Israel's bitter enslavement.

Why do we recline at the table?

In ancient times, reclining symbolized freedom. Since our spiritual forefathers were liberated on this night, we recline as a sign of their and our freedom.

We can rejoice that in His death we have found life. In Messiah's coming is the Passover completed.

We, too, who are believers in Messiah, can rejoice that we can celebrate the Passover in the days of our Messiah, Yeshua. We celebrate that in Him we transition from death to life. In Christ, the essence of Passover is fulfilled.

Makkot – Second Cup: The Cup of Judgment

Guest #1:

God appointed Moses to free the Israelites from Egyptian bondage. His mission was to demand their release from Pharaoh, enabling them to worship the God of Israel. God warned Moses of Pharaoh's likely resistance:

"But I know that the king of Egypt will not let you go unless a mighty hand compels him. So I will stretch out my hand and strike the Egyptians with all the wonders that I will perform among them. After that, he will let you go." (Exodus 3:19,20)

Guest #2:

Each of Moses' pleas to Pharaoh for Israel's release was met with refusal, prompting God to send a series of plagues, escalating in severity. Pharaoh's heart hardened further with each calamity. After ten devastating plagues, the last being the most grievous, Pharaoh finally yielded. About this final plague, it is written:

"On that same night I will pass through Egypt and strike down every first-born—both men and animals—and I will bring judgment on all the gods of Egypt. I am the LORD." (Exodus 12:12)

Each Passover cup symbolizes a full cup of joy, except for the second cup—the Cup of Plagues—because God teaches us never to rejoice over the fate of our enemies. In Proverbs 24:17-18, we are reminded, *"Do not gloat when your enemy falls; when he stumbles, do not let your heart rejoice, or the LORD will see and disapprove and turn his wrath away from him."*

As believers in Yeshua, our joy is tempered by recognizing the great cost of redemption. A far greater price was paid for our redemption from Satan's bondage (Hebrews 2:14-15; Colossians 2:13-15).

We will now recite the Ten Plagues Egypt suffered due to Pharaoh's hardened heart, a reminder that one person's bad decision can cause much pain. As we do so, we dip our little finger into the cup, letting a drop of wine fall (onto a napkin or plate), symbolically reducing the fullness of our cup of joy this night.

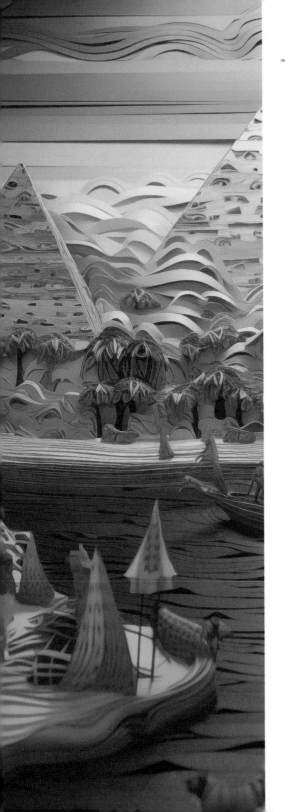

Blood

Frogs

Gnats

Flies

Livestock

Boils

Hail

Locusts

Darkness

Firstborn

"Dayenu" – It Would Have Been Enough

In light of our redemption, we acknowledge God's goodness. For each act of mercy and kindness, we declare "Dayenu!" which means "it would have been sufficient!"

Leader:	*Everyone:*
- Had He brought us out from Egypt *And not judged them.*	*Dayenu!*
- Had He judged them *And not judged their idols.*	*Dayenu!*
- Had He judged their idols *And not slain their first-born.*	*Dayenu!*
- Had He slain their first-born *And not given us their property.*	*Dayenu!*
- Had He given us their property *And not divided the sea for us.*	*Dayenu!*
- Had He divided the sea for us *And not brought us on dry ground.*	*Dayenu!*
- Had He brought us on dry ground *And not drowned our oppressors.*	*Dayenu!*

Leader:	**Everyone:**

– Had He drowned our oppressors
And not helped us forty years in the desert.

Dayenu!

– Had He helped us forty years in the desert
And not fed us manna.

Dayenu!

– Had He fed us manna
And not given us the Sabbath.

Dayenu!

– Had He given us the Sabbath
And not brought us to Mount Sinai.

Dayenu!

– Had He brought us to Mount Sinai
And not given us the Torah.

Dayenu!

– Had He given us the Torah
And not brought us into the Land of Israel.

Dayenu!

– Had He brought us to the Land of Israel
And not built us the Holy Temple.

Dayenu!

All: **Dai-dai-yenu, dai-dai-yenu, dai-dai-yenu, dayenu, dayenu!** **x2**

[Everyone lifts up the reduced second cup. Leaning to the left.]

Everyone:

" *Blessed are you, O Lord our God, King of the universe, Creator of the fruit of the vine.*

Amen!

Leader:

The Lamb Shankbone

The Passover offering, eaten by our spiritual forefathers during temple times, had a significant purpose. It was because the Holy One, blessed be He, spared our forefathers in Egypt. As it is written in Exodus 12:26-27:

"And when your children ask you, 'What does this service mean to you?' you shall say, 'It is the Passover sacrifice to the Lord, for He passed over the houses of the people of Israel in Egypt when He struck the Egyptians but spared our houses.'"

In relation to the Messiah, it is prophesied in Isaiah 53:7:

"He was oppressed and afflicted, yet He did not open His mouth; He was led like a lamb to the slaughter, and as a sheep before its shearers is silent, so He did not open His mouth."

And, in John 1:29:

"John saw Jesus coming toward him and said, 'Look, the Lamb of God, who takes away the sin of the world!'"

The lamb shankbone symbolizes the Temple sacrifice and sits on the Passover plate as a reminder of the first Passover lamb sacrificed for the children of Israel. Its blood was applied to the lintels and doorposts of their homes. We lift the shankbone of the lamb, recalling the lamb slain for the firstborn males among the Jewish people. This moment also leads us to reflect upon the death of Jesus, the Lamb of God, who takes away the sin of the world (John 1:29). The blood of Christ acts as a spiritual detergent, washing us clean. Through His selfless act, we receive forgiveness of sins and, in turn, are called to extend forgiveness to others!

Matzah – Unleavened Bread

We eat this matzah; what is its significance? It is because our spiritual forefathers' dough did not have time to rise when the Holy One, blessed be He, redeemed them. Exodus 12:39 says, ***"They baked unleavened cakes of the dough because they had been driven out of Egypt and did not have time to prepare food for themselves."***

The matzah is unleavened, symbolizing purity, being without sin or blameless. In its baking, it is pierced and striped, illustrating the Messiah, who was without sin yet was pierced and striped: ***"But He was pierced for our transgressions, He was crushed [humbled] for our iniquities; the punishment that brought us peace was on Him, and by His wounds, we are healed."*** (Isaiah 53:5)

Maror – Bitter Herbs

We eat this bitter herb; why do we do so? It is because the Egyptians embittered the lives of our spiritual ancestors in Egypt, as written in Exodus 1:11-14: *"They put slave masters over them to oppress them with forced labor... but the more they were oppressed, the more they multiplied and spread; so the Egyptians came to dread the Israelites and worked them ruthlessly. They made their lives bitter with harsh labor in brick and mortar and with all kinds of work in the fields; in all their hard labor, the Egyptians worked them ruthlessly."*

The bitter herb reminds us of the sorrow, persecution, and suffering of Israel throughout the generations. Therefore, we are bound to thank, praise, laud, glorify, extol, honor, bless, exalt, and revere Him who performed all these miracles for our spiritual fathers and us. He brought us from slavery to freedom, from sorrow to joy, from mourning to festivity, and from servitude to redemption. Let us, therefore, sing a new song in His presence!

If you'd like, this is a great opportunity to sing a worship song.

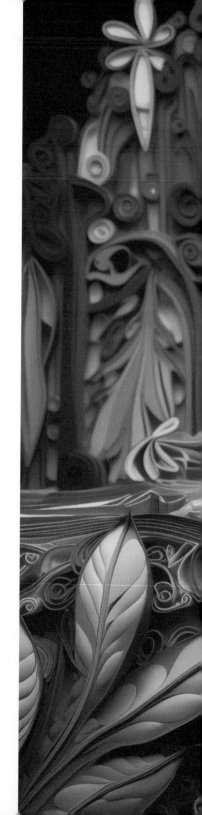

As the first portion of the Seder draws to a close, the family engages with several remaining elements on the Seder plate. These elements are designed to engage our senses in recalling the Passover story. Each one symbolizes a distinct aspect of Israel's journey from slavery to freedom. For believers in Yeshua, these elements also symbolize the journey from spiritual bondage to liberation in the Messiah. We raise the matzah tash and together recite the following blessing:

Blessed are you, O Lord our God, King of the universe, who brings forth bread from the earth.

Each person now breaks off a small piece of matzah.

Charoset – Fruits and Nuts

The charoset, a sweet mixture, symbolizes the mortar used by the children of Israel to make bricks while laboring under Pharaoh's harsh taskmasters. It is traditionally eaten with matzah. To resolve a debate about the proper way to observe Passover, Rabbi Hillel, a renowned sage, initiated the tradition of the "Hillel sandwich." This is made by combining the maror (bitter herbs) and charoset between two pieces of matzah. This mix of bitter and sweet serves as a reminder that, even in times of sorrow, God's promise can bring joy.

Beitzah – Roasted Egg

The roasted egg on the Seder plate is a reminder of the daily Temple sacrifice, which can no longer be offered since the Temple no longer stands. During the Passover Seder, Jewish people are reminded that there is currently no sacrifice to bring about righteousness before God. We take a piece of the egg and dip it in salt water, symbolizing tears.

We will take Rabbi Hillel's idea one step further. Each person will take pieces of matzah, charoset (sweet mixture), maror (bitter herb), and Beitzah (egg), and put them together.

– All eat together –

It's time to
serve the
Passover meal

Enjoy your food and share many personal stories of redemption!

Tzafun – the Afikoman

After the meal, the Seder leader sends the children to find the afikoman, the middle piece of matzah that was broken, wrapped, and hidden earlier by the leader.[1] The finder brings it to the leader, who redeems it with a reward.

The leader then unwraps the afikoman, blesses it, and breaks it into olive-sized pieces, distributing them to everyone.

Leader:

For believers in Yeshua, this is a significant moment, recalling when Yeshua revealed His identity and coming sacrifice, as noted in Luke 22:19: ***"This is My body which is given for you; do this in remembrance of Me."***

Yeshua, likened to the afikoman, symbolizes the mediator between God and people. His death, burial, and resurrection are mirrored in the afikoman ritual, representing His perfect sacrifice.

1. Kids, I hope for you he didn't forget! (Eitan)

When the Seder leader unwraps the afikoman and distributes it, it reminds us that Yeshua the Messiah shared His life with all who believe. Now, the leader will break the afikoman into olive-sized pieces, giving one to each guest. As you hold it, reflect on Yeshua's sacrifice. Then, all partake in **communion** together after saying the following prayer together:

Blessed are you, O Lord our God, King of the universe, who brings forth bread from the earth.

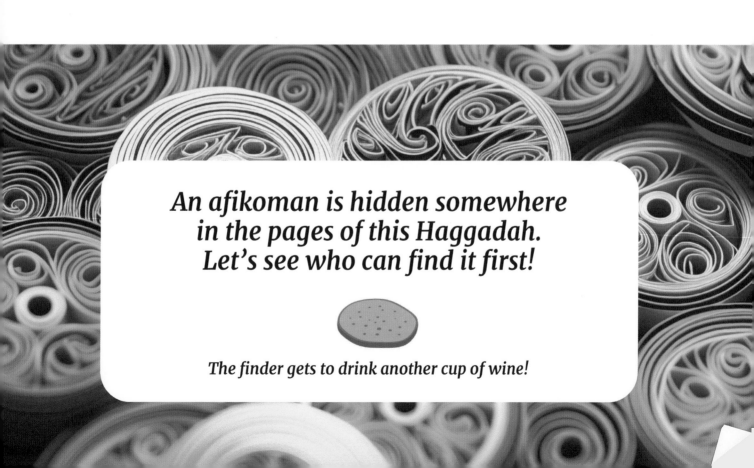

An afikoman is hidden somewhere in the pages of this Haggadah. Let's see who can find it first!

The finder gets to drink another cup of wine!

HaGeulah – Third Cup: The Cup of Redemption

The Cup of Redemption, grounded in God's promise from Exodus 6:6, *"I will redeem you with an outstretched arm and with great judgments,"* serves as a reminder of the lamb's blood, symbolizing the price of Israel's redemption. Similarly, Yeshua likely referred to this cup when He said in Luke 22:20, *"This cup which is poured out for you is the new covenant in My blood."* Here, He alluded to a redemption greater than what the Israelites experienced in Egypt – the redemption and deliverance of humanity through the blood of the Lamb of God. Yeshua's words echo the New Covenant prophecy from Jeremiah 31:31–34.

Once everyone's cup is filled, the following blessing is recited together while leaning to the left:

"Blessed are you, O Lord our God, King of the universe, Creator of the fruit of the vine."

Amen!

Eliyahu – Elijah's Cup

The Bible, in Malachi 4:5, foretells Elijah's appearance to announce the coming of the Messianic King:

"Behold, I am going to send you Elijah the prophet before the coming of the great and terrible day of the Lord."

During Passover, it is a tradition to set an additional place, complete with a cup for Elijah. The Seder leader often sends a child to the front door to look for Elijah. To date, Elijah has not physically attended a Seder.

Or did he?! The Bible, in Luke 1:17, referring to John the Baptist, states, *"It is he who will go as a forerunner before Him in the spirit and power of Elijah."* John came in the spirit of Elijah to herald the first coming of the Messiah, a role fulfilled by Yeshua.

Hallel – Fourth Cup: The Cup of Praise

The appropriate response to redemption is joy. We celebrate, mindful of the deliverance of the Jewish people from Egyptian slavery and the redemption of both Jewish and Gentile followers of the Messiah from the bondage of sin and death. The fourth and final cup of the Passover Seder, the Cup of Praise, symbolizes rejoicing, joy, and fulfillment. It represents the initial experience of freedom that follows redemption. This cup also serves as a reminder of Israel's promised future beyond Egyptian slavery—a future of freedom in the Promised Land. Furthermore, it anticipates the glorious future for Israel and the world in the era of the Messianic kingdom.

Once everyone's cup is filled, all lift it, and the following blessing is recited together. However, now that you are mostly drunk, you should be able to recite the blessing in Hebrew! ;)

"Baruch Atah Adonai Eloheinu Melech HaOlam, Bohre Pri HaGahfen."

Amen!

Hallel Psalms

In a spirit of joy and gratitude, we celebrate all that God has done for us. He has liberated us from slavery, redeemed us, and drawn us close to Him. We offer Him our heartfelt praise! As our Seder concludes, we joyfully sing one of the Hallel Psalms (Pss. 113–118), echoing the tradition observed even by Yeshua in His final moments of fellowship with His disciples, as they too sang after their Seder (Matt. 26:30; Mark 14:26).

Psalm 114 / Everyone:

" *When Israel came out of Egypt, Jacob from a people of foreign tongue, Judah became God's sanctuary, Israel his dominion.*

The sea looked and fled, the Jordan turned back; the mountains leaped like rams, the hills like lambs.

Why was it, sea, that you fled? Why, Jordan, did you turn back? Why, mountains, did you leap like rams, you hills, like lambs?

Tremble, earth, at the presence of the Lord, at the presence of the God of Jacob, who turned the rock into a pool, the hard rock into springs of water."

Next Year in Jerusalem!

Traditionally, the Seder concludes with a collective and jubilant declaration of hope and faith, recited together:

"L'Shana HaBa'ah B'Yerushalayim!"

("Next Year in Jerusalem!")

If you found value in this Haggadah, I'd be deeply grateful if you could spare a moment to leave a rating on Amazon. Your feedback and support would be immensely appreciated. Moreover, if you're keen to delve deeper into Israel and Judaism through a Jewish–Christian lens, you might find the following books particularly enriching:

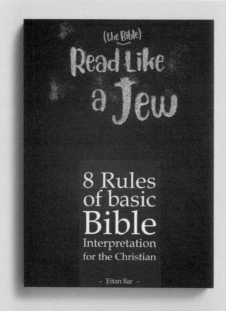

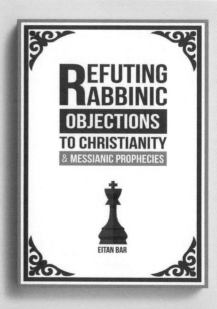

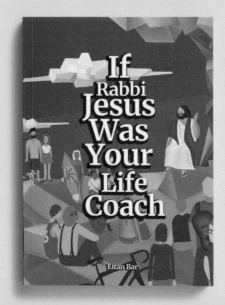

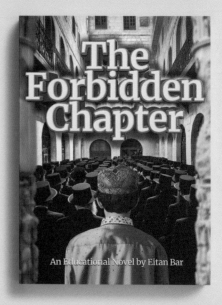

Printed in Great Britain
by Amazon

43365107R00027